A Character Building Book ™

Learning About Fairness from the Life of
Susan B. Anthony

Kiki Mosher

The Rosen Publishing Group's
PowerKids Press ™
New York

Published in 1996 by The Rosen Publishing Group, Inc.
29 East 21st Street, New York, NY 10010

First Edition

Book design: Erin McKenna

Photo credits: Cover © Archive Photos; pp. 4, 11, 19 © AP/Wide World Photos; p. 7 © Michael Lichter; pp. 8, 12, 15 © Corbis-Bettman; pp. 16, 20 © The Bettmann Archive.

Mosher, Kiki.
    Learning about fairness from the life Susan B. Anthony / by Kiki Mosher.
        p.   cm. — (A character building book)
    Includes index.
    Summary: A brief biography examining the idea of fairness in the life of the woman known for her efforts to secure the right to vote for women.
    ISBN 0-8239-2422-X
    1. Anthony, Susan B. (Susan Brownell), 1820–1906—Juvenile literature. 2. Feminists—United States—Biography—Juvenile literature. 3. Suffragists—United States—Biography—Juvenile literature. 4. Fairness—Juvenile literature. [1. Anthony, Susan B. (Susan Brownell), 1820–1906. 2. Feminists. 3. Women—Biography. 4. Fairness.] I. Title. II. Series.
    HQ1413.A55M68 1996
    305.42'092—dc20   96-16089
    [B]   CIP
                                                                                 AC

Manufactured in the United States of America

Table of Contents

The Fight for Fairness

Susan Brownell Anthony was born in Adams, Massachusetts, in 1820. Even as a child, Susan believed that all people should be treated **equally** (EE-kwul-ee). But most people didn't agree with her. Most people thought that women and **slaves** (SLAYVZ) were not equal to white men. Susan knew this was not fair. She knew everyone was equal.

◀ *Susan led the fight for women's right to vote.*

Growing Up

Susan's family belonged to the Religious Society of Friends. They were **Quakers** (KWAY-kerz). Quakers believed that all men and women should be treated equally. Susan's parents followed Quaker practice. They treated all eight of their children equally. They also taught their children to express their own **opinions** (uh-PIN-yunz). Susan grew up believing that she should say what she thought. She also believed she and her sisters deserved the same opportunities as her brothers.

Susan grew up following the Quaker belief that men and women are equal. ▶

Education

In 1826, the Anthony family moved to Battensville, New York. Mr. and Mrs. Anthony sent all of their children to school there. In the early 1800s, it was unusual for parents to send their daughters to school. Once in school, Susan realized that not everyone thought that men and women should be treated equally. Her teacher was one of those people. Susan once asked him why he taught long division to boys but not to girls. He said that girls didn't need those skills! Susan knew better. She asked another student to teach her long division. And he did.

◀ *Susan was treated unfairly as a student. As a teacher, she treated all her students equally.*

Unfairness to Women

Susan grew up to become a teacher. She liked her job, but she was angry when she learned that male teachers were paid four times as much as she was. Susan also knew that few girls were allowed to go to high school or college. This meant that only men could do certain jobs, like being doctors. Women were supposed to work at home. Everything a woman owned became her husband's as soon as she married him. And although women were more than half the **population** (pop-yoo-LAY-shun), they did not have the right to vote.

Women who fought for the right to vote looked for support in many areas, including in the schools. ▶

The Spirit of Change

These **inequalities** (IN-ee-KWAL-ih-teez) were all based on whether someone was a man or a woman. They angered Susan, who knew they were unfair. She wanted to do something to change them.

Susan was used to fighting for human rights. Along with her father, she had been an **abolitionist** (ah-boh-LISH-un-ist). That meant that she believed that **slavery** (SLAY-ver-ee) was wrong and should be outlawed. Susan wanted to help end slavery. But she wasn't allowed to—because she was a woman.

◀ *Sometimes women were allowed to watch meetings on issues such as ending slavery. But they were rarely, if ever, allowed to say what they thought at these meetings.*

Changing the Rules

Because she was kept out of men's meetings, Susan decided to start a women's group to work on important issues such as ending slavery. Many women joined her. In 1851, Susan met Elizabeth Cady Stanton. Elizabeth was a writer. She, too, had started her own women's group. Her group fought for equal rights for all people. Susan and Elizabeth became friends and partners in working for women's rights. They fought for women's **suffrage** (SUF-rej), or women's right to vote. But many Americans thought equal rights for women was a bad idea.

Susan B. Anthony and Elizabeth Cady Stanton helped convince the public that women were equal to men, and that they had rights. ▶

Hard Work

Susan became a great speaker. She appeared before **Congress** (KON-gres). There she asked lawmakers to change laws that treated girls and women as second-class **citizens** (SIT-ih-zenz). She helped create groups promoting women's rights. Susan started a newspaper about women's suffrage called *The Revolution*. Elizabeth wrote and edited articles for the newspaper.

Susan devoted all her time to her cause. Long train rides, bad food, and cold hotel rooms did not discourage her.

◀ *One way women showed their support for the fight for women's right to vote was by marching in protests.*

Public Ridicule

Many people did not agree with Susan's work. Her ideas were new, and some people were afraid of them. Could women be equal to men? What would that mean? Many Americans agreed that slaves should be free and equal. But the idea of women being **independent** (in-dee-PEN-dint) was scary for some. Men and even women made fun of Susan. They called her names. They wrote mean things about her in newspapers. But she did not give up.

Although some people were afraid of Susan's ideas, many supported them. ▶

The Elections

In 1872, Susan convinced officials to let her and her three sisters vote in the presidential election. But Susan was arrested soon after. The judge at her trial said it was against the law for women to vote. He said she had broken the law. He fined her $100. Susan refused to pay the fine, but the judge released her anyway. The fine is still unpaid today.

Susan's arrest brought the subject of women's suffrage to public attention. At last, people began to understand the importance of women gaining the right to vote.

Women were finally granted the right to vote in 1920. Thanks in part to Susan, women now have a way to make sure they are treated fairly and equally.

The Right to Vote

American women were granted the right to vote in 1920, 100 years after Susan was born. Susan didn't live to see the results of her work. She died in 1906. But her efforts to change public opinion of women changed history.

In 1979, Americans honored Susan by putting her image on the new dollar coin. Susan B. Anthony became the first American woman to appear on a coin. She will always be remembered for her courage and strength in the fight for fairness.

Glossary

abolitionist (ah-boh-LISH-un-ist) Person who believes that slavery should be outlawed.

citizen (SIT-ih-zen) Member of a country.

Congress (KON-gres) Law-making part of the government of the United States.

equal (EE-kwul) To have the same value as someone or something else.

independent (in-dee-PEN-dint) Thinking or acting for yourself.

inequality (IN-ee-KWAL-ih-tee) Being unequal in value.

opinion (uh-PIN-yun) What a person thinks.

population (pop-yoo-LAY-shun) The people that make up a group.

Quaker (KWAY-ker) Member of the Religious Society of Friends.

slave (SLAYV) Person who is owned by someone else.

slavery (SLAY-ver-ee) Practice of allowing some people to "own" others.

suffrage (SUF-rej) The right to vote.

Index